the first summer study book for bass

by cassia harvey
edited by matthew roberts

CHP189

©2007 by C. Harvey Publications All Rights Reserved.

www.charveypublications.com - print books
www.learnstrings.com - PDF downloadable books
www.harveystringarrangements.com - chamber music

Bass Note Chart

G string

D string
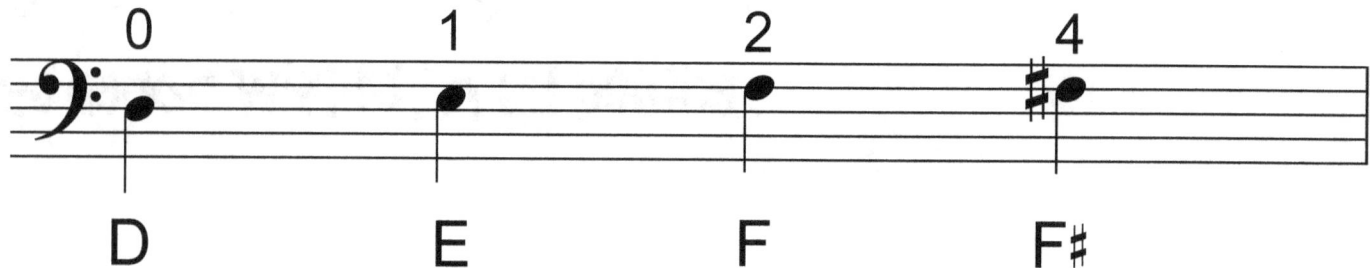

A string
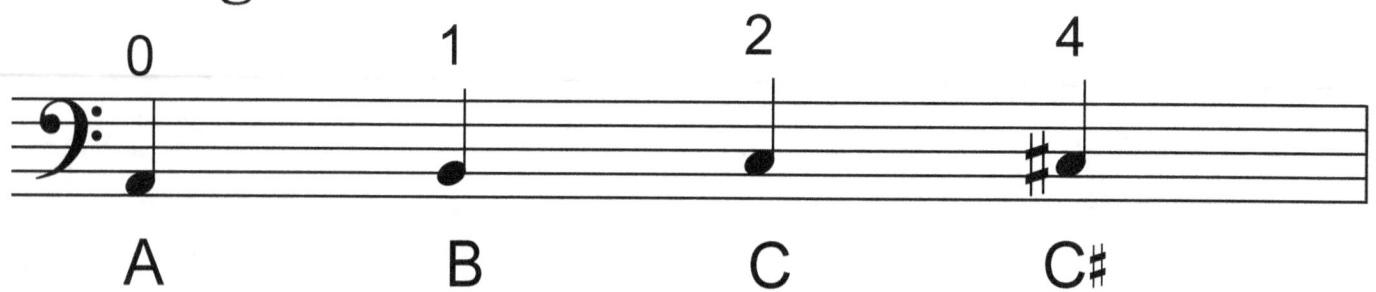

E string

©2007 C. Harvey Publications All Rights Reserved.

by Cassia Harvey
edited by Matthew Roberts

1. No more flimsy first fingers!

2. Cripple Creek

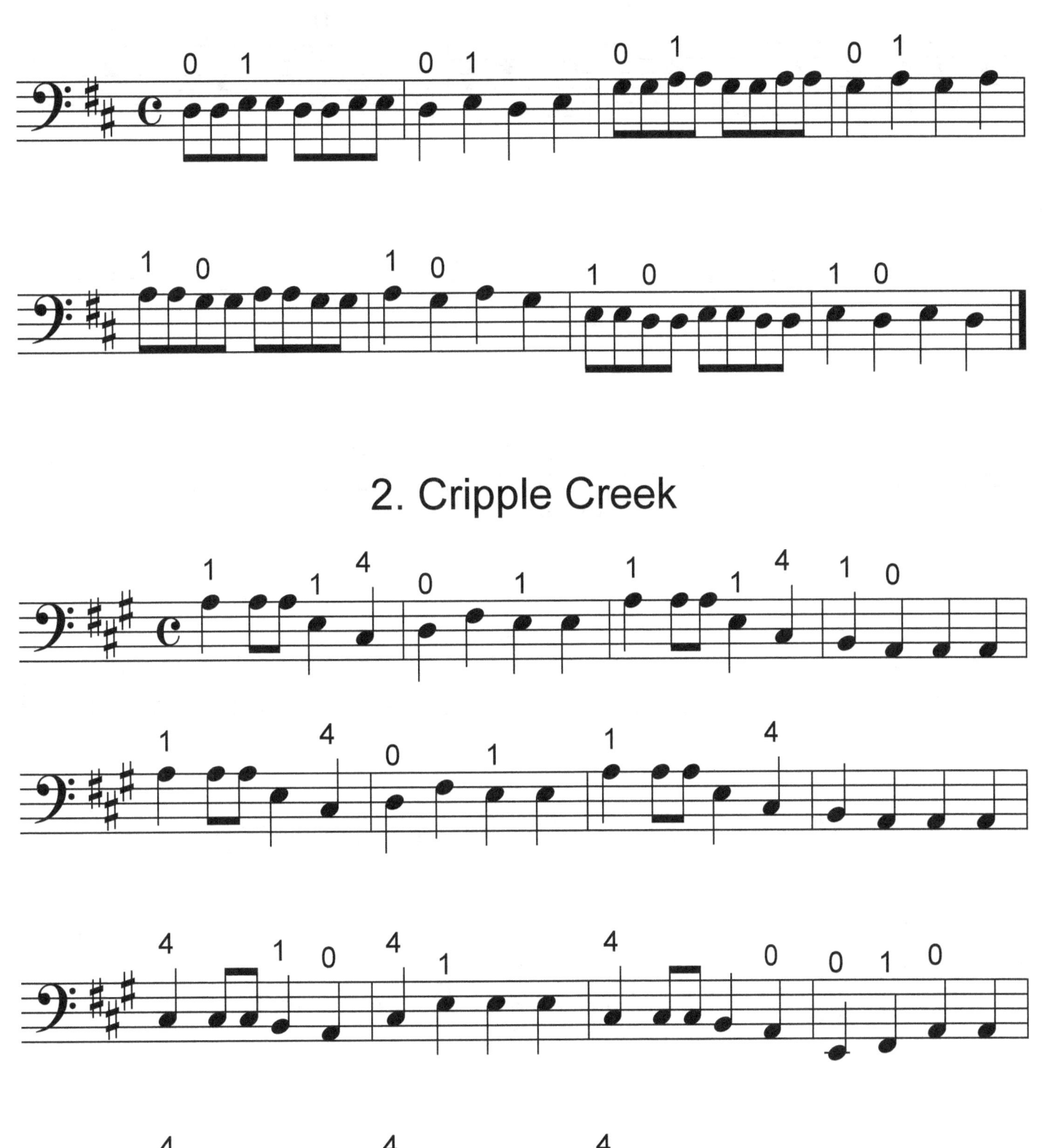

©2007 C. Harvey Publications All Rights Reserved.

3. What Do You Do With a Drunken Sailor?

4. Drunken Sailor String Crossing

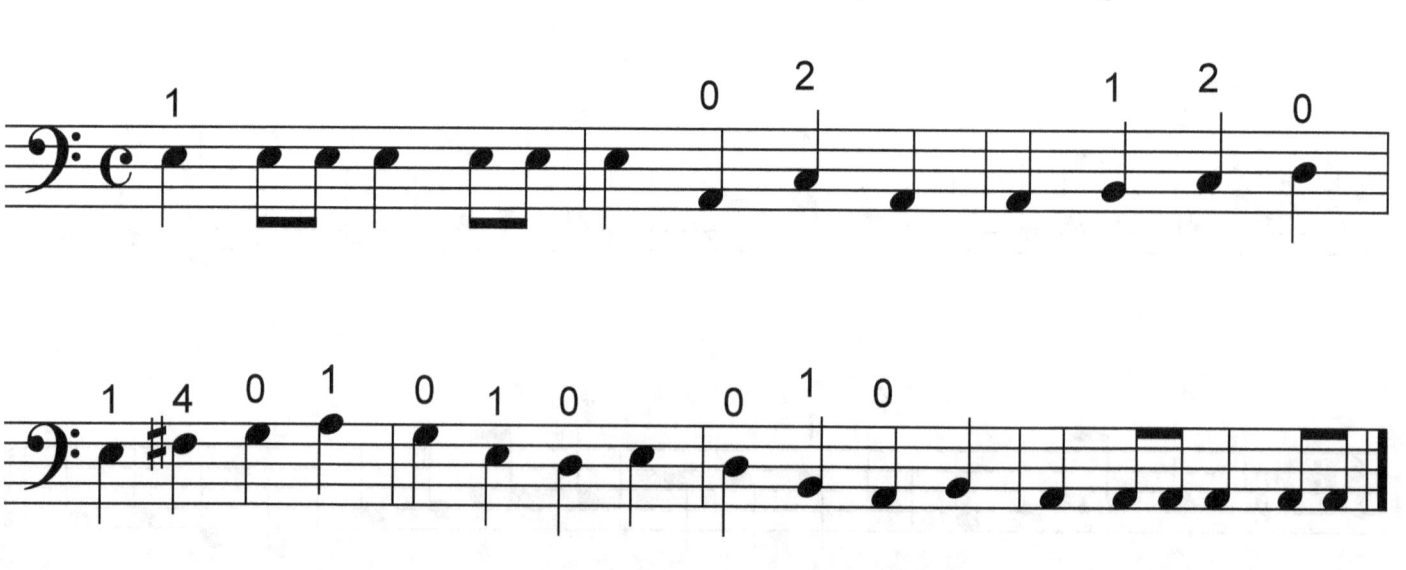

©2007 C. Harvey Publications All Rights Reserved.

5. Fiddle Tune

6. Rossini's William Tell

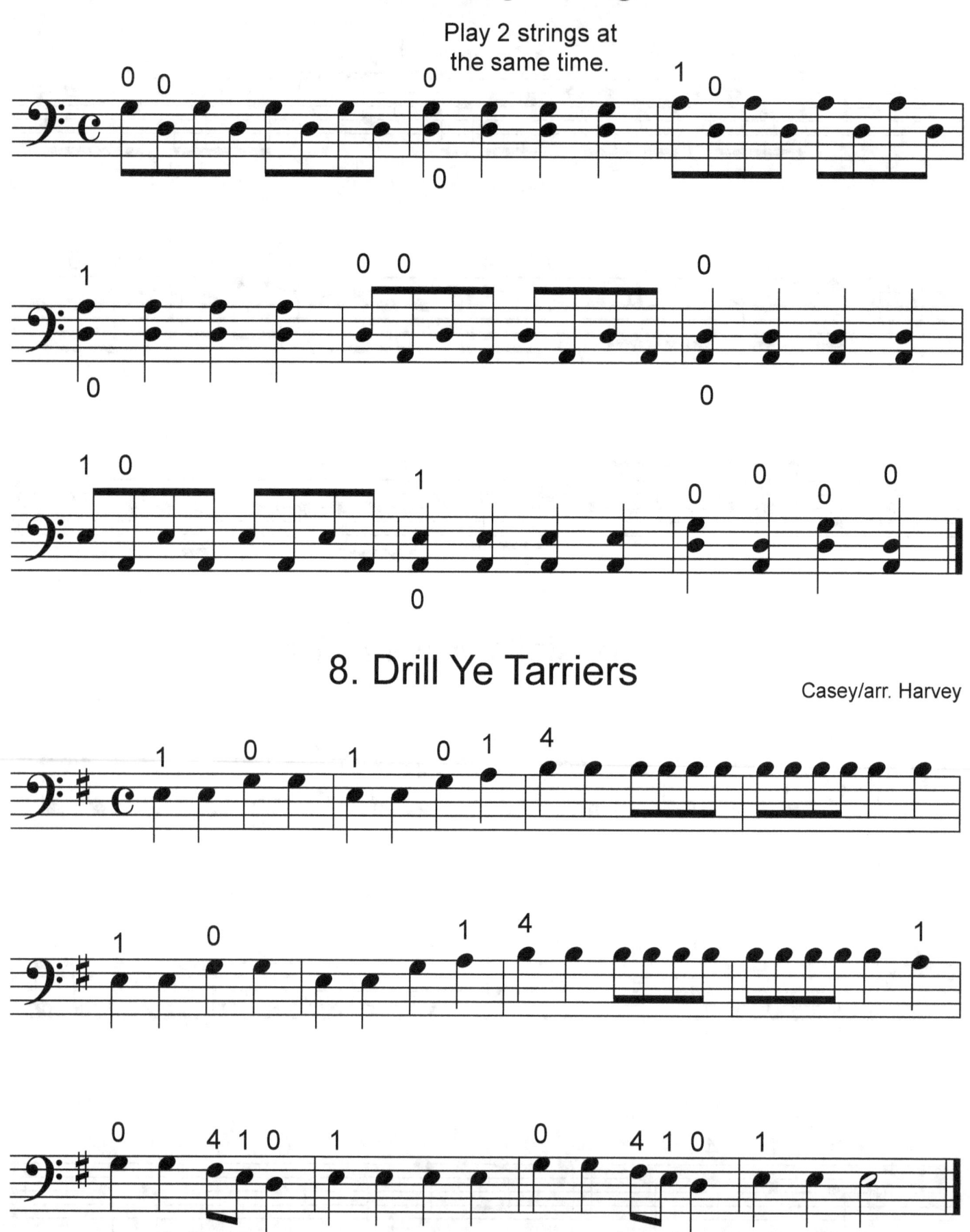

9. Oh Susannah

Foster/arr. Harvey

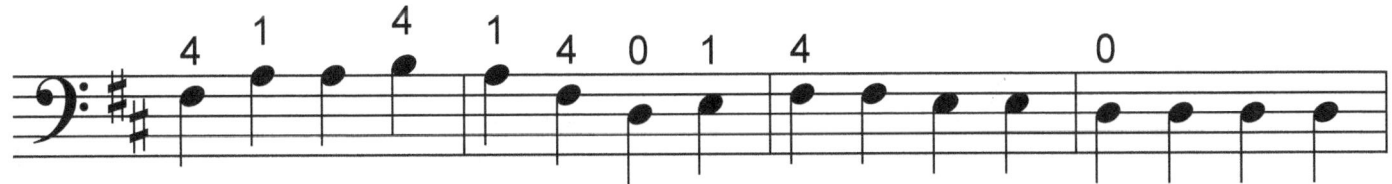

10. Susannah's Exercise

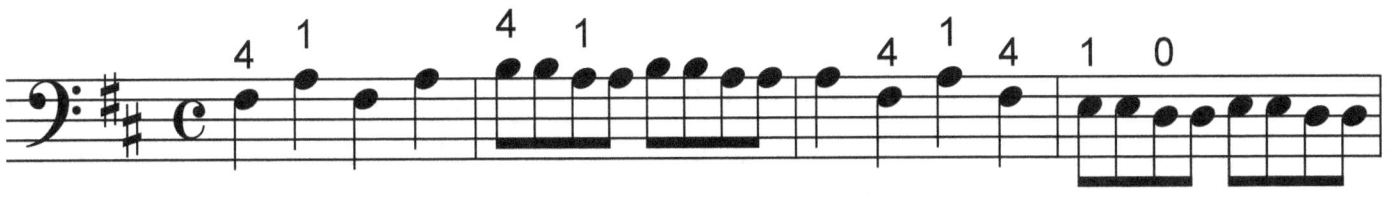

©2007 C. Harvey Publications All Rights Reserved.

11. Mountain Exercise

12. She'll Be Comin' Round the Mountain

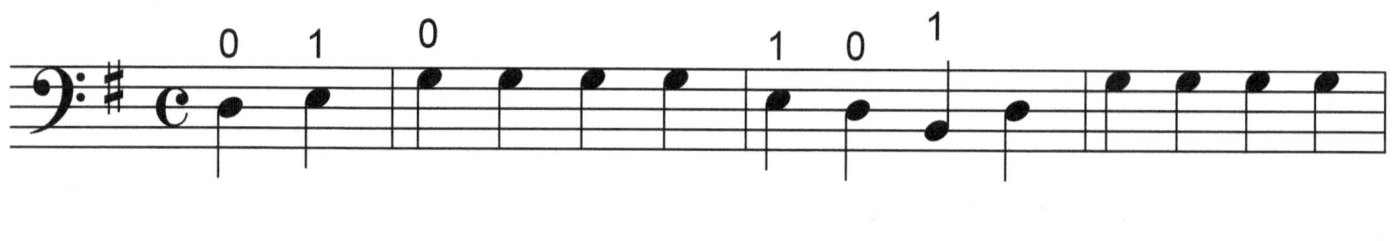

©2007 C. Harvey Publications All Rights Reserved.

13. Sleep Exercise

14. Are You Sleeping?

15. Sleeping Yet?

©2007 C. Harvey Publications All Rights Reserved.

16. Finger Trainer

17. Michael, Row the Boat Ashore

18. Find the Hidden Songs

19. Bugler's Exercise

20. Reveille Bugle Call

21. Bugler's Next Exercise

22. Assembly Bugle Call

22. Taps Bugle Call

Remember: A dotted half note gets 3 counts.

©2007 C. Harvey Publications All Rights Reserved.

23. Finger Running

24. Swallowtail Jig

©2007 C. Harvey Publications All Rights Reserved.

25. Playing on E and A

26. Buffalo Gals

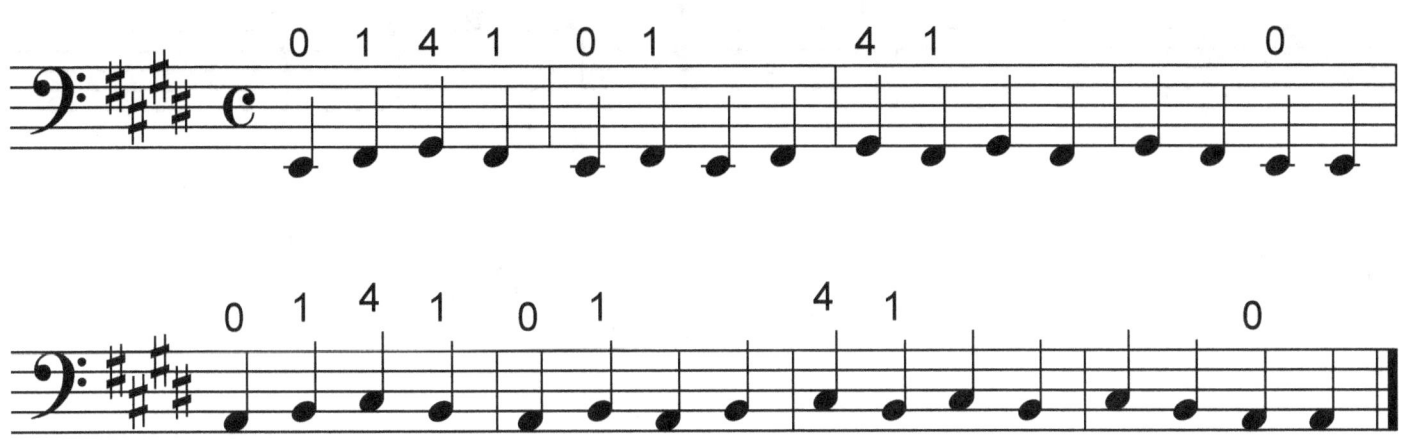

27. Blow the Man Down

28. Arpeggios

29. On Top of Old Smoky

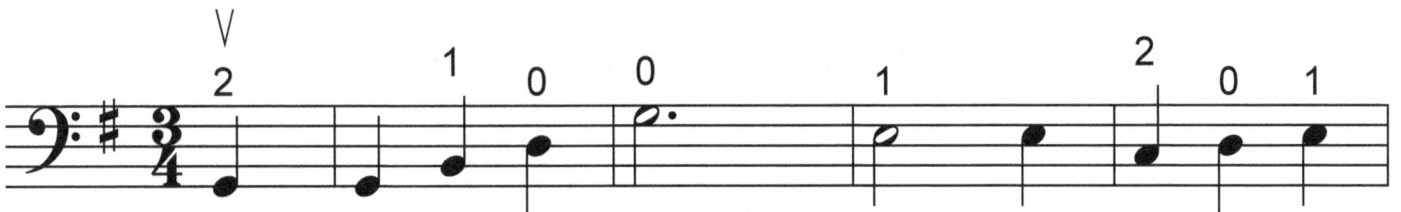

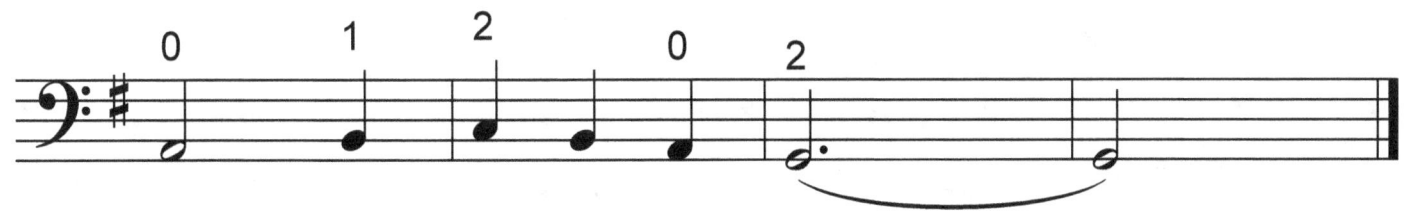

©2007 C. Harvey Publications All Rights Reserved.

30. Summer Fiddle

31. Snake Charmer's Dance

©2007 C. Harvey Publications All Rights Reserved.

32. This Old Man

33. Double Trouble

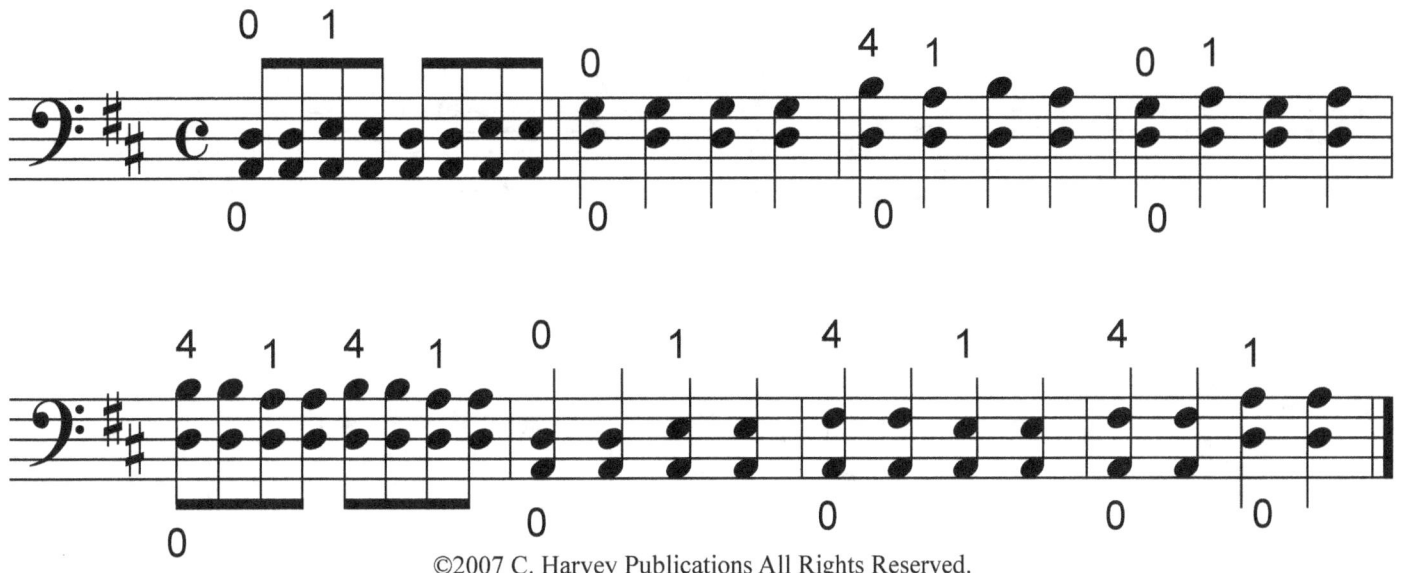

©2007 C. Harvey Publications All Rights Reserved.

34. String Crossing

35. Simple Gifts

©2007 C. Harvey Publications All Rights Reserved.

40. Home on the Range

Kelley/arr. Harvey

©2007 C. Harvey Publications All Rights Reserved.

41. Hail to the Chief

Kelley/arr. Harvey

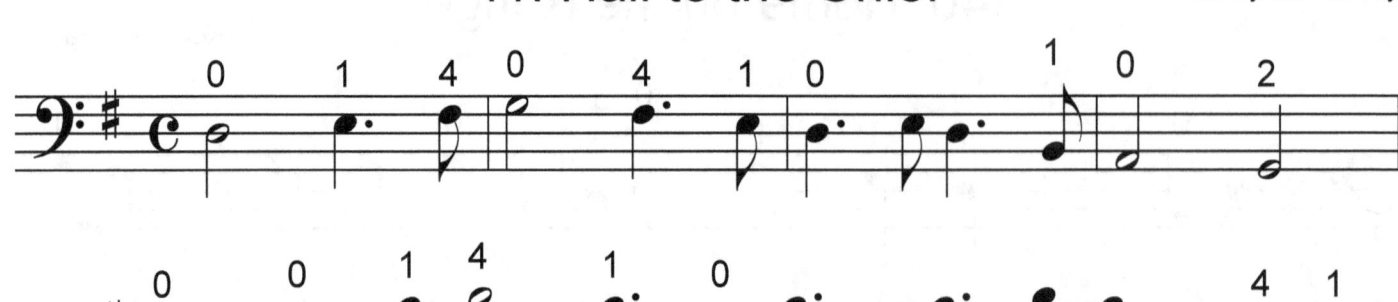

42. Yankee Doodle

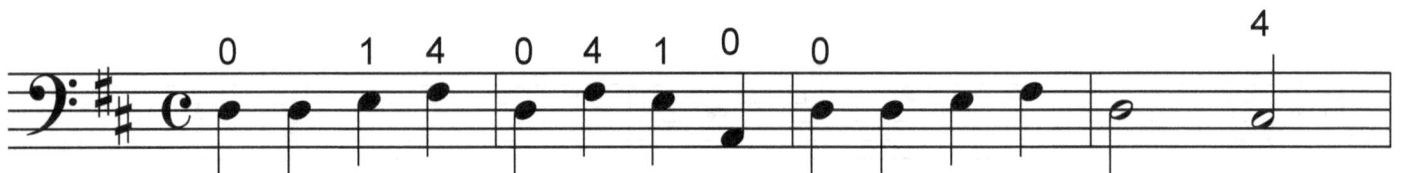

©2007 C. Harvey Publications All Rights Reserved.

www.ingramcontent.com/pod-product-compliance
Lightning Source LLC
Chambersburg PA
CBHW080039100526
44584CB00023BA/3690